## WHAT THE LITTLE PIG SAW

What the little pig saw
When he went round the world
Caused his ears to stick up
And his tail to be curled.

*For*

HOWARD WALLER

*Bon voyage, my friend,*
*may the fourth be with you.*

First published 1999 by
Walker Books Ltd
87 Vauxhall Walk, London SE11 5HJ



This book has been typeset in
Monotype Bembo and McNaughton Pirate Schoolbook.

Printed in Hong Kong

British Library Cataloguing in Publication Data
A catalogue record for this book is
available from the British Library.

ISBN 0-7445-4970-1

Colin McNaughton

# WISH YOU WERE HERE (AND I WASN'T)

*A Book of Poems and Pictures for Globe Trotters*



WALKER BOOKS
AND SUBSIDIARIES
LONDON • BOSTON • SYDNEY

# WISH YOU WERE HERE

Dear All,

The sea looks great, but I've not tested –
   Locals say it's shark-infested.
Beach looks fine, I'm not complaining –
   Go there, soon as it stops raining.
The food's okay, if you like fish –
   And things that crawl across your dish.
As for our hotel, it's neat –
   It should be great when it's complete.
I'll bring you back a souvenir –
   Goodbye for now, wish you were here.

(And I wasn't!)

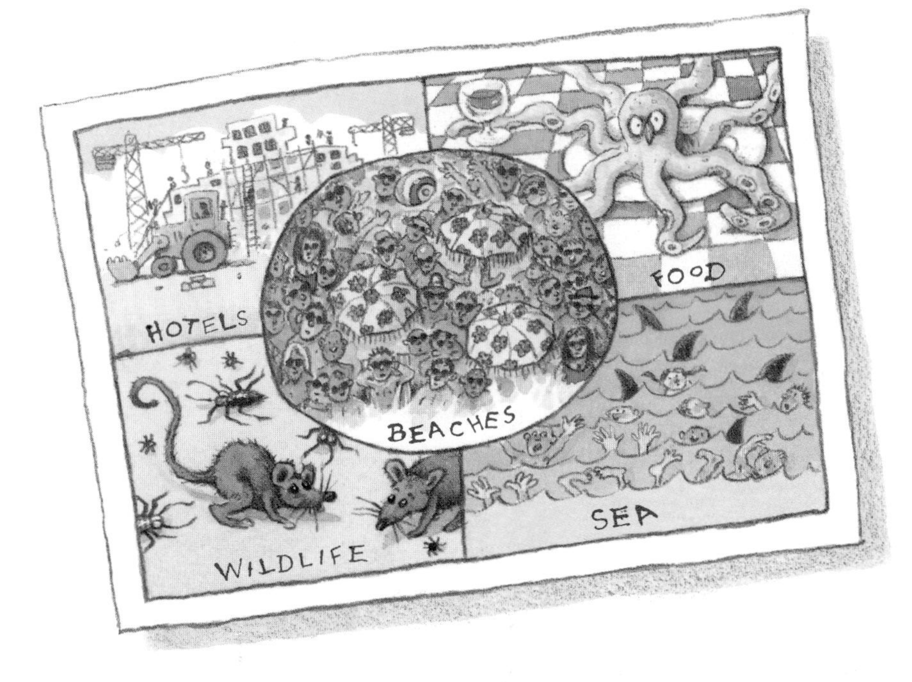

## THE OOZILY WOOZILY PLONK

There's the Hairily Scarily Donk
And the Heavily Devily Conk.
But none is as weird
Or so horribly feared
As the Oozily Woozily Plonk.

He likes nothing more than a chat,
But I'd strongly advise against that!
Just get on your bike
Because you wouldn't like
What the Plonk means by "chewing the fat".

It is awfully bad manners, I know,
But just make your excuses and go.
No, don't even smile,
Run a four-minute mile
If a Plonk says so much as "Hello!"

Should a Plonk ever hunt you and find you,
He'd certainly crush you and grind you.
But there's nothing to fear,
There are none around here...

GOOD HEAVENS, THERE'S ONE

RIGHT BEHIND YOU!!!!!!!!!!!!!!!!

# I'M OFF TO TREASURE ISLAND

*The first verse is the chorus and can be repeated*
*after every verse – depending on how silly you're feeling.*

Ooh-aargh, avast, ha-har!
Ooh-aargh, avast, ha-har!
I'm off to Treasure Island,
Ooh-aargh, avast, ha-har!

Most folks go to Blackpool,
To Spain or Turkey, but,
I'm off to Treasure Island –
I'm a Treasure Island nut!

I'll sail the *Hispaniola*,
A cutlass at my side;
I'm off to Treasure Island
On the early morning tide.

I'll curse an' spit, me hearties!
I'll tame the wildest sea!
I'm off to Treasure Island –
It's a pirate's life for me!

I'll fly the Jolly Roger,
Better stay out of me way!
I'm off to Treasure Island,
I'll be gone by break of day!

"Pieces of eight!" cries Captain Flint.
"There is no pirate bolder!"
I'm off to Treasure Island
With a parrot on me shoulder.

I'll follow Billy Bones's map,
Meet up with old Ben Gunn.
I'm off to Treasure Island –
Gonna have some pirate fun!

I'll sail home with me treasure,
  As rich as rich can be.
I'm off to Treasure Island –
  Do you want to come with me?

Yo-ho-ho an' a bottle of rum,
  Treasure Island here I come!
Long John Silver'd better run –
  I'm off to Treasure Island!

# YET ANOTHER POEM TO SEND TO YOUR WORST ENEMY

Juggins, muggins,
Gowk, galoot.
Noodle, nutcase,
Nincompoop.
Smarmy, barmy,
Featherbrain.
See through you like
Cellophane.
Raving, rambling,
Round the bend.
A brain transplant
I'd recommend.
Drivelling, snivelling,
"Looney Tunes".
IQ of a set of spoons.
You really haven't got a clue,
Thick as two short planks are you.
Join the monkeys in the zoo.
Yours sincerely, toodle-oo.

## THE ARMCHAIR TRAVELLER

The armchair traveller drifts away
And takes a path he's often trod.
He gently strolls through fields of dreams,
A rambler in the Land of Nod.

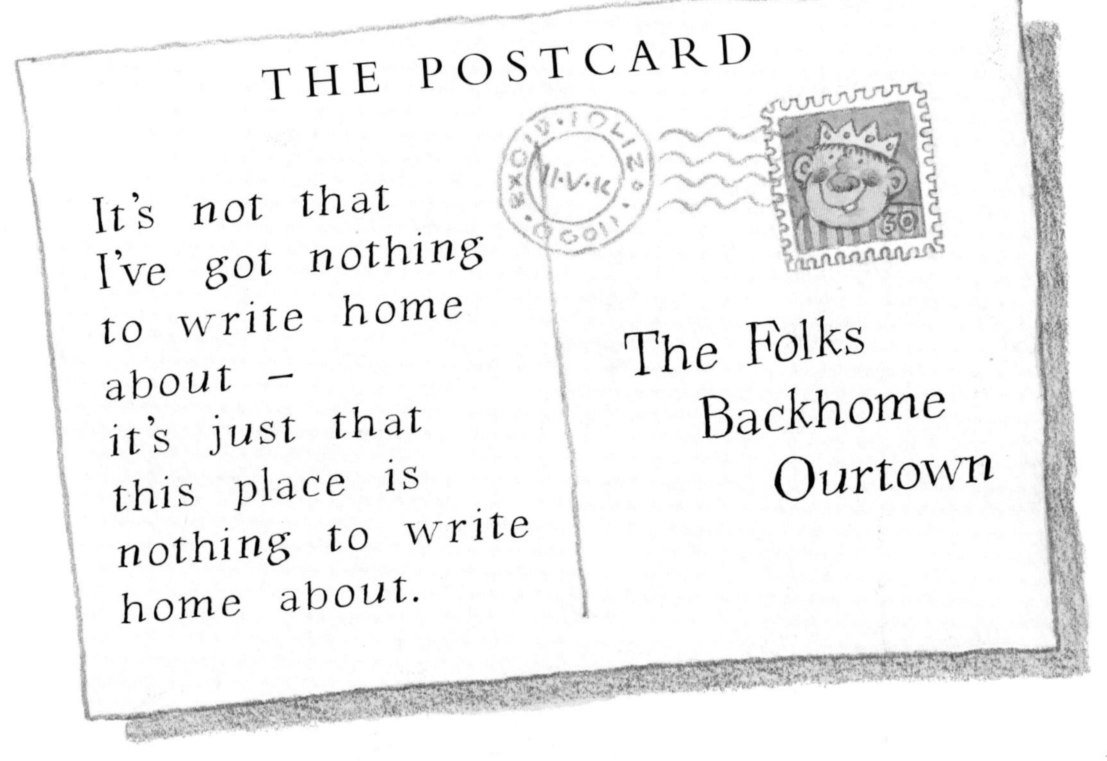

# THE NOMAD RUSH

If in the desert you should be
And men on camels you should see
Going slowly, that would be
The famous Nomad Rush.

Through the desert dunes they ramble,
Drag their feet and sort of shamble,
Never rise above an amble.
That's the Nomad Rush.

They gaze into the clear blue sky
And half asleep they mosey by.
Now and then they'll maybe sigh.
That's the Nomad Rush.

They take their time, go nice 'n' easy.
Ooze on by, so cool and breezy.
Easy-peasy, lemon-squeezy –
That's the Nomad Rush.

## IF I COULD FLY LIKE ICARUS

If I could fly like Icarus
I'd really have some fun.
I'd pack a little suitcase
And fly off to the sun.

I'd fly so high, I'd kiss the sky,
The clouds would be my bed.
I'd swoop so low, I'd call your name
And plop upon your head!

I'd fly around the world and back,
Yes, life would be a hoot.
I wouldn't change a thing, except –
I'd pack a parachute!

# A STING IN THE TAIL

Two explorers, one called Splong
(The other's name is Snit),
Meet by chance on a jungle path
And chew the fat a bit.

Says Splong to Snit, "Please help me, do,
For something puzzles me.
I've just seen something very strange
Descending from a tree.

The body's pink, has purple stripes,
With orange spots beneath.
The head is large, the mouth is huge,
With great big pointy teeth.

From head to toe, this thing has spines,
And legs, I counted nine.
It partly slithers, partly crawls,
And leaves a trail of slime.

I've travelled this world over,
Seen all there is to see,
But I've never seen the likes of this.
I think you will agree."

"Pull the other one," says Snit.
"I don't believe a word!
It's quite the most preposterous thing
That I have ever heard!

There's no such insect, bird or beast.
You take me for a fool?"
But Splong, he does not take offence,
Just smiles and keeps his cool.

"So what do you call this mythical beast?"
Sceptical Snit, he snorts.
"I've simply no idea," says Splong,
"But one just crawled
up the leg of your shorts."

# ALL I ASK IS A PERFECT DAY

All I ask
  Is a perfect day
On a perfect beach
  In a perfect bay

In the perfect shade
  Of a perfect tree
With a perfect view
  Of a perfect sea

With a perfect breeze
  And a perfect sky
Read a perfect book
  Swat a perfect fly.

In a perfect pool
  Find a perfect shell
Eat a perfect peach
  With a perfect smell

Skim a perfect stone
  Dig a perfect hole
Catch a perfect wave
  Score a perfect goal

Make a perfect dive
  See a perfect fish
With a perfect tail
  Give a perfect swish.

Then in this perfect world
  Meet a perfect friend
And bring this perfect day
  To a perfect end.

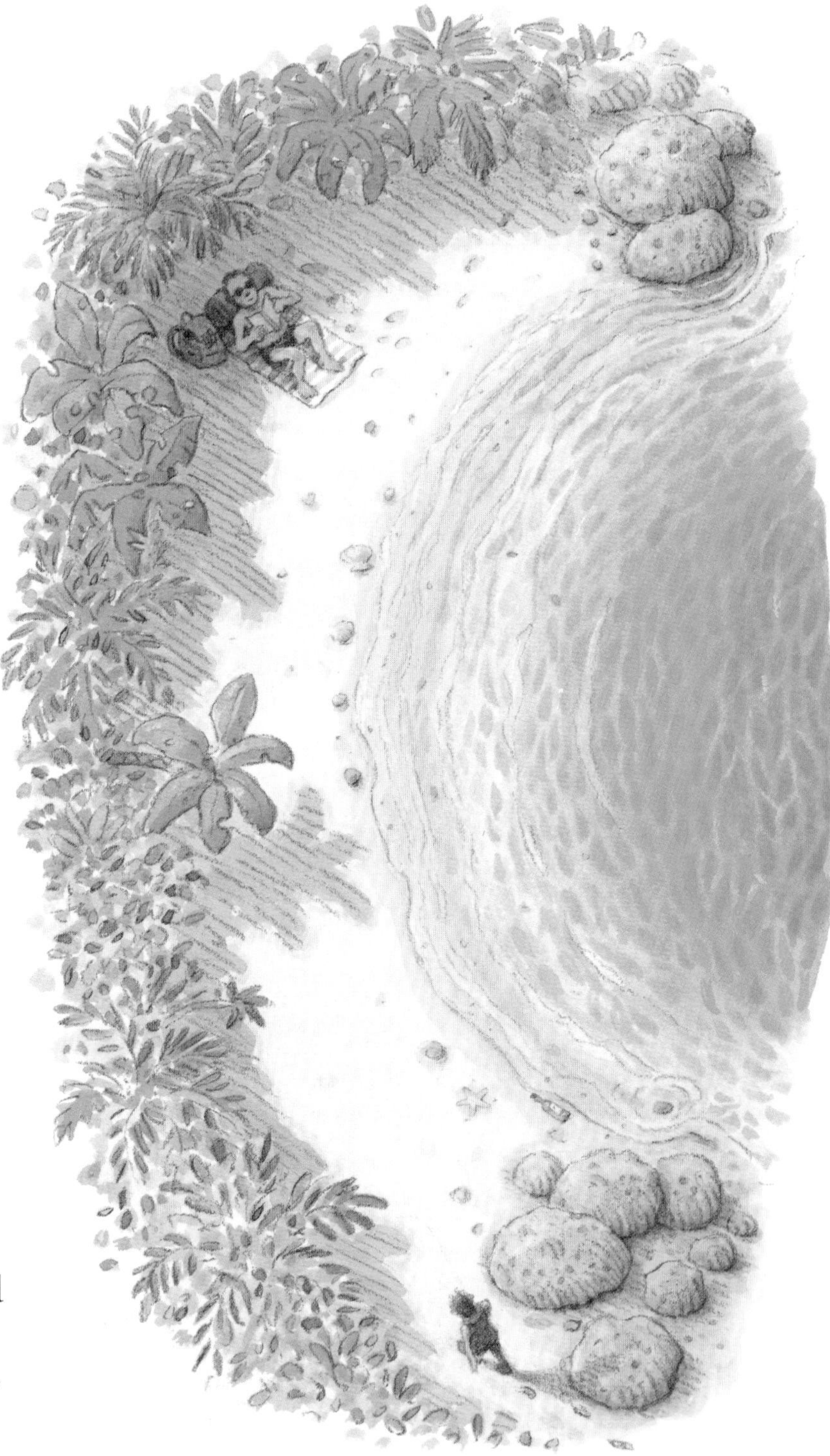

# A SAD CASE

# ROW, ROW, ROW YOUR BATH

Row, row, row your bath,
Gently down the stream.
Pull the plug and watch your bath
Become a submarine.

Row, row, row your bath,
Smile and pull the plug.
Merrily, merrily, merrily, merrily,
Glug-glug-glug-glug-glug.

## COUNTING ON YOU
### (A Love Letter)

Love me WANDA,
    Love me TWODA,
Love me THREEDA,
    Love me FOURDA,
Love me FIVEDA,
    Love me SIXDA,
Love me SEVENDA,
    Love me EIGHTDA,
Love me NINEDA,
    Love me TENDA, do!

# IF YOU'RE TRAVELLING IN TRANSYLVANIA

If you're travelling in Transylvania
And you're all alone one night
And there's a terrible hammering on your door
And you wake with a terrible fright
And you open your door and standing there
Is a figure pale and green –
If he claims to be Count Dracula …
Just pray it's Hallowe'en!

# FIRST DRAFT OF THE MOST FAMOUS AUSTRALIAN SONG EVER

Once a jolly swagman
Camped by a billabong
Under the shade of a coolabah tree.
He unpacked his wallaby
And fired up his goolagong.
"Who'll come a-waltzing with Hilda and me?

Waltzing the builder,
Waltzing St Kilda,
Who'll come a-waltzing with Hilda and me?"
And he danced and he sang
As he waited till his billy boiled.
"Who'll come a-waltzing with Hilda and me?"

And as that jolly swagman
Waited till his billy boiled
Under the shade of the coolabah tree,
A man-eating crocodile
Wearing nothing but a smile,
Jumped from the billabong and bit him on the knee.

Oh, waltzing the builder … etc.

I'm a Possum.
I'm a Cuscus.
I'm a Currawong and I'm a bird. So What!
I'm a Fruit bat.
I'm a Long-nosed Bandicoot.
I'm a little Oomphmax.
I'm a Sugar Glider.
I'm a Koala and I'm not a bear!
I'm a Tree Kangaroo.
CENSORED
I'm a cat called Henry and I shouldn't really be here.
I'm a Tasmanian Devil.
G'day! I'm a Crocodile.
I'm a Tasmanian Tiger and I'm supposed to be extinct. Ha!
I'm a Rusty Numbat.
I'm an Echidna.
I'm a Wobbly – I mean a Wallaby.

# WELL I HAVE!

Ever been lost in the Australian bush?
Ever been trekking in the Hindu Kush?
Ever gone skiing, got slush in the mush?
Well I have!

Ever got stuck on a mountainside?
Ever jumped a gap that was just too wide?
Ever got caught by an incoming tide?
Well I have!

Ever been sick on an aeroplane?
Ever been soaked by a monsoon rain?
Ever been caught in a hurricane?
Well I have!

Ever bounced across the sea in a hovercraft?
Ever sailed across a pond on a home-made raft?
Ever thrown a pebble down an old mine shaft?
Well I have!

Ever caught a catfish in the South of France?
Ever been swimming in your underpants?
Ever been bitten by giant ants?
Well I have!

Ever spent the day on a perfect beach?
Ever opened your shirt and discovered a leech?
Ever dived for a shell that was just out of reach?
Well I have!

Ever walked for hours in a rainforest gloom?
Ever found a cockroach in your hotel room?
Ever swam with stingrays in a blue lagoon?
Well I have!

Ever climbed a pyramid in Mexico?
Ever seen what you thought was a UFO?
Ever seen a shark from a pedalo?
Well I have!

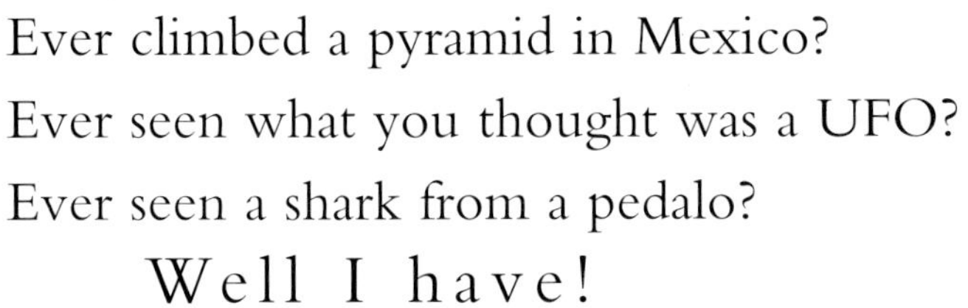

Ever had a scorpion inside your shoe?
Ever pat the head of a kangaroo?
Ever take the hippy trail to Katmandu?
Well I have!

Ever run full speed down a giant dune?
Ever swam in the sea by the light of the moon?
Ever found that holidays end too soon?

WELL I HAVE!

## NO ROOM TO SWING A CAT!

My hotel room was tiny.
No room to swing a cat.
My cat was overjoyed and said
"Well, thank the Lord for that!"

# FISHING FOR COMPLIMENTS

I've been fishing for Compliments
with baited breath
in the river of life.
So far I've caught:
a "My, what a clever boy",
a "Hi, handsome",
a "What a man" and
a "You're really funny".

I did catch a Small Insult
but I threw it back.

## MISS MELANIE MISH

Here is a picture of Melanie Mish
She hails from the planet of Flong.
Weighs nine hundred kilos and smells of old fish,
If you think that she's ugly – you're wrong!

For before you, you see the most beautiful Flonger
The planet of Flong's ever seen.
If you think that she's ugly, you couldn't be wronger.
Meet Melanie Mish – BEAUTY QUEEN!

MISS FLONG

# I JUST DON'T BELIEVE IN AEROPLANES

I've flown round this world of ours several times.
I've gobbled the food and I've guzzled the wines.
I've sat watching cabin staff doing their mimes
But I just don't believe in aeroplanes.

I've had it explained to me time and again,
Aeronautical experts have all tried in vain,
But I can't take it in 'cause the whole thing's insane!
I just don't believe in aeroplanes.

"It's simple," they say, to persuade me to shift,
"The action of airflow on wings causes lift."
It's round about then that my mind comes adrift!
I just don't believe in aeroplanes.

What pushes me over the brink of despair
Is you fly through the clouds on a wing and a prayer,
Supported by ten thousand metres of – AIR!
I just don't believe in aeroplanes.

Here's what we're looking at, here is the deal:
That four hundred tons of plastic and steel
Can float through the air, well excuse me – get real!
I just don't believe in aeroplanes.

## UNDER A CLOUD

The sun is shining everywhere
  Except above my head.
I think the best thing I could do
  Is spend the day in bed.

## SUMMER IS THE SILLY SEASON

Summer is the silly season,
  Everyone goes mad.
Everyone takes off their clothes,
  Even Mum and Dad!

# ARE WE NEARLY THERE YET?

*To be read in a monotonous drone of a voice. Start reciting this poem right at the beginning of a journey and just carry on and on and on and on and on… Please adapt to suit circumstances: "Daddy are we there yet?" and so on.*

Mummy are we there yet,
Are we nearly there?
Mummy are we there yet,
Are we nearly there?
Mummy are we there yet,
Are we nearly there?
Mummy are we there yet,
Are we nearly there?
Mummy are we there yet,
Are we nearly there?
Mummy are we there yet,
Are we nearly there?
Mummy are we there yet,
Are we nearly there?
Mummy are we there yet,
Are we nearly there?
Mummy are we there yet,

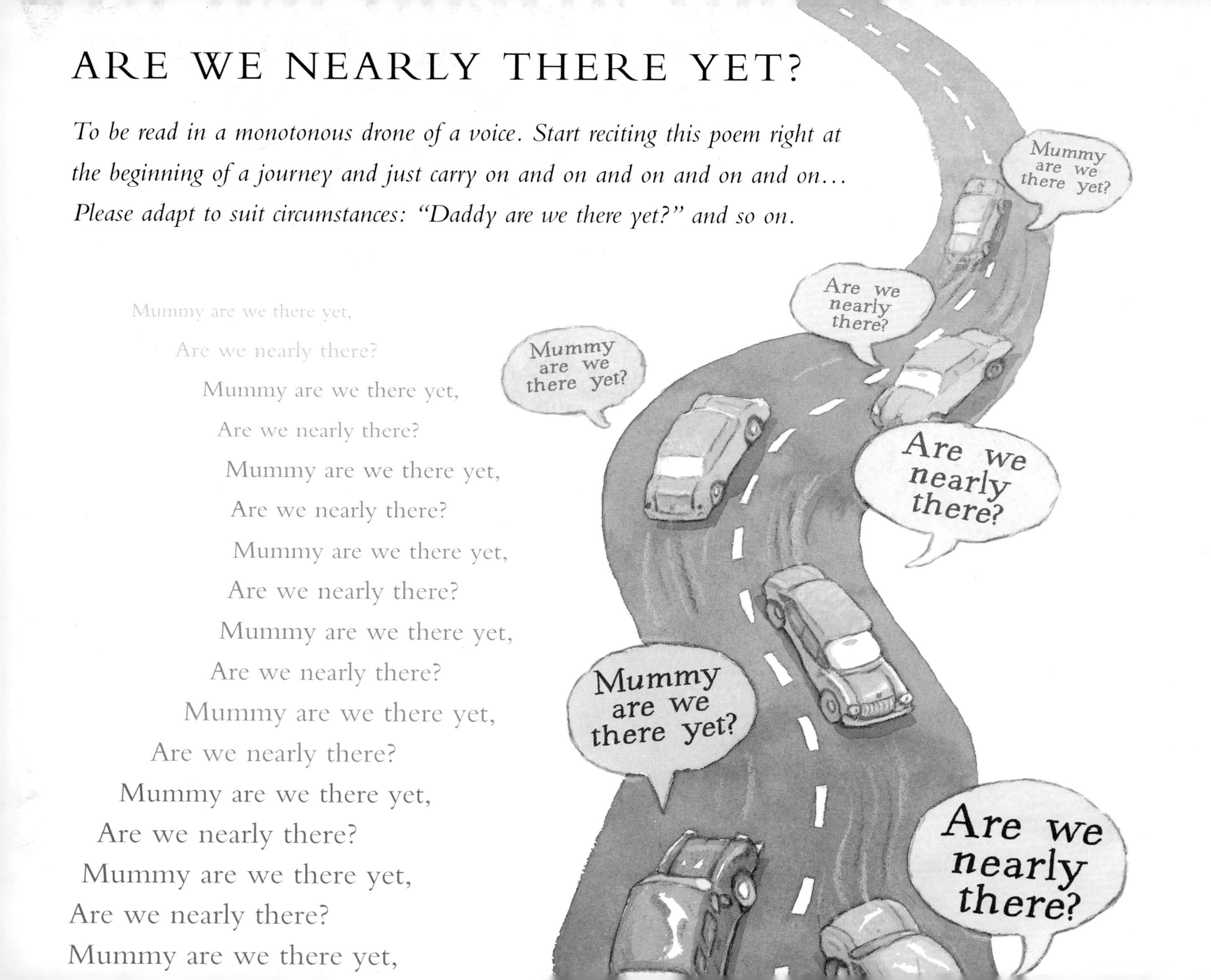

Mummy are we there yet?

Are we nearly there?

Are we nearly there?
Mummy are we there yet,
Are we nearly there?
Mummy are we there yet,
Are we nearly there?
Mummy are we there yet,
Are we nearly there?
Mummy are we there yet,
Are we nearly there?
Mummy are we there yet,
Are we nearly there?
Mummy are we there yet,
Are we nearly there?
Mummy are we there yet,
Are we nearly there?
Mummy are we there yet,
Are we nearly there?
Mummy are we there yet,
**Are we nearly there?**
**Mummy are we there yet,**
**Are we nearly there?**
**Mummy are we there yet,**
**Are we nearly there?**
**Mummy are we there yet,**
**Are we nearly there?**

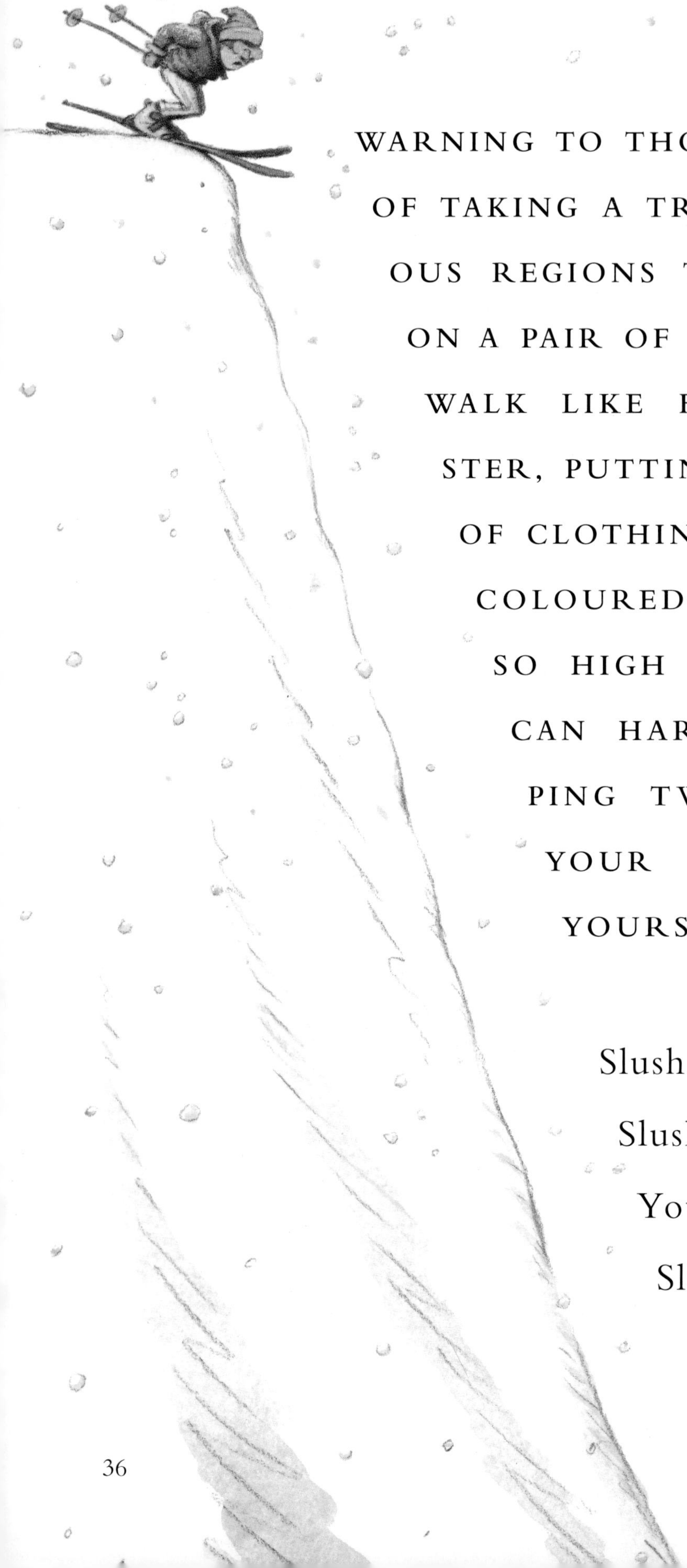

WARNING TO THOSE PERSONS THINKING OF TAKING A TRIP TO THE MOUNTAINOUS REGIONS THIS WINTER, PULLING ON A PAIR OF BOOTS THAT MAKE YOU WALK LIKE FRANKENSTEIN'S MONSTER, PUTTING ON FIFTEEN LAYERS OF CLOTHING TOPPED BY A MULTICOLOURED ROMPER-SUIT, GOING SO HIGH UP A MOUNTAIN YOU CAN HARDLY BREATHE, STRAPPING TWO HUGE PLANKS TO YOUR FEET AND PUSHING YOURSELF OFF THE TOP:

Slush in the mush,
Slush in the mush.
You'll just end up with
Slush in the mush.

# GETTING CARRIED AWAY

I was sitting out back in my rocking-chair,
Just passing the time of day.
When a terrible wind done picked me up
And I got carried away.

It carried me over the mountains
And dropped me in the bay.
A humpbacked whale came sailing by
And I got carried away.

It carried me over the ocean
With its billowy salty spray.
It flipped me into the eye of a storm
And I got carried away.

The storm blew high and mighty,
A swirl of leaden grey.
It dumped me into the back of a truck
And I got carried away.

That truck went over the prairies
Where the dear old anchovies play.
It flicked me on to the back of a horse
And I got carried away.

Well, I rode home and told my mum
Where I had been all day.
She shook her head and then she said:
"Oh, you do get carried away,
Sometimes,
You do get carried away."

# I FEEL SICK!

Set off before dawn, sick,
Feeling very, yawn, sick,
Wish I'd not been born, sick,
I FEEL SICK!

Is it very far, sick,
Ate a chocolate bar, sick,
Feeling very car-sick,
I FEEL SICK!

Corner of my eye, sick,
Trees are flashing by, sick,
Wish that I could die, sick,
I FEEL SICK!

Dad says look ahead, sick,
Wish that I was dead, sick,
Take me home to bed, sick,
I FEEL SICK!

Queasy, woozy, hot, sick,
My brother says I'm not sick,
Thanks a rotten lot, sick,
I FEEL SICK!

Twisty, turny road, sick,
Chocolate overload, sick,
Ready to explode, sick,
I FEEL SICK!

Daddy, hurry up, sick,
Feel it coming up, sick,
Hic! Hiccup! Hiccup! Sick!
I'VE BEEN SICK!

## P. S.

Didn't make the door, sick.
Threw up on the floor, sick.
There isn't any more sick.

I FEEL FINE!

# LEMMY WAS A PILOT

Lemmy was a pilot,
A top-notch pilot,
Lemmy was a pilot,
Six years old.

Lemmy flew around the world,
*All* the way around the world,
Single-handed 'round the world,
Go, Lemmy, go!

Lemmy in the pilot's seat
Didn't stop to drink or eat,
Had a record time to beat,
Go, Lemmy, go!

Beat the record easily
But boy did Lemmy need to pee
(It rained that night on Tennessee),
Go, Lemmy, go!

And at the height of Lemmy's fame,
Lemmy quit the flying game –
Lemmy found it much too tame,
Go, Lemmy, go!

Now Lemmy is an astronaut,
An outer-space-type astronaut,
The fly-across-the-cosmos sort.
Go, Lemmy, go!

## THE TEACHER'S HOLIDAY LAMENT

Goodbye blue skies,
Hello rain.
Just got back
From a month in Spain.

Goodbye new friends
Left behind.
Hello back to
Daily grind.

Goodbye hotel
Swimming pool.
Goodbye beaches,
Hello school.

Hello puddles,
Goodbye sea.
Hello grey skies,
Poor old me.

Hello clouds,
Goodbye sun.
Hello school,
Goodbye fun.

Goodbye hours
Of peace and quiet.
Hello daily
Classroom riot.

*(Yes, I know this poem goes on a bit, but then so do some teachers I know.)*

## SEA SAW ME

When I was three I went to see
The sea and let the sea see me.
Sea see me see me see sea.
I saw the sea and the sea saw me.

## AAAAHHHRREEAAAHHREEEAAA – OUCH!

Tarzan's recovering,
Coming on fine.
We're close to discovering
Who greased the vine.

## FOOT SLOGGING

Our teacher, striding out in front,
Shouts: "Walking's good for us!"
The kids, as one, all answer back:

WE'D RATHER TAKE THE BUS!

## A FLIGHT OF FANCY

I planted a packet of birdseed
In a line as straight as an arrow.
I didn't get much in the way of a crop,
Just a parrot, two ducks and a sparrow.

# STROLLIN' DOWN THE HIGHWAY LEAVIN' HOME TRAVELLIN' BLUES

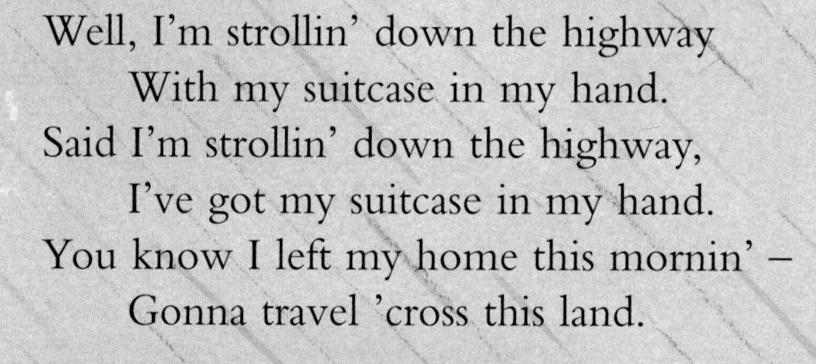

Well, I'm strollin' down the highway
With my suitcase in my hand.
Said I'm strollin' down the highway,
I've got my suitcase in my hand.
You know I left my home this mornin' –
Gonna travel 'cross this land.

Well, I'm strollin' down the highway,
You know I've left my mom an' dad.
Said I'm strollin' down the highway,
You know I've left my mom an' dad.
When they find I'm missin' –
Boy, will they be mad.

Yeah, I'm strollin' down the highway
An' the rain is in my shoes.
Strollin' down the highway,
Rain is sloppin' in my shoes.
You know I'm feelin' mighty lonesome –
Yeah, I've got those travellin' blues.

Strollin' down the highway,
Got my teddy by my side.
Strollin' down the highway,
Got my teddy by my side.
I ain't never goin' home again –
You know a fella's got his pride.

I'm strollin' down the highway
When a car begins to slow.
Said I'm strollin' down the highway
When a car begins to slow.
This guy looks down an' smiles at me –
Says, "Where you wanna go?"

Well, I'm ridin' down the highway,
My strollin' days are done.
Yeah, I'm ridin' down the highway,
Yeah, my strollin' days are done.
My mommy's in the back seat –
Sayin', "We sure missed you, son."

I'm ridin' down the highway
An' I've lost the urge to roam.
Yes, I'm ridin' down the highway,
An' I've lost that urge to roam.
I look up at the driver …
An' say, "Daddy, take me home."

# IT'S A SMALL WORLD

*(The first paragraph from my forthcoming science-fiction novel.)*

"It's a small world," said the Mega-Ultimate-Space-Beast as he potted the Earth into a black hole; making it six straight wins. The Mega-Ultimate-Space-Beast Universal Galaxy Pool All-Comers Championship was his. OK, so it was a crummy little competition, held in a stinking backwater, but he was young and who knew what the future held in store…

# FRANKENSTEIN'S MONSTER WORLD TOUR

I left my heart in San Francisco,
My torso in Nepal,
My arms in Valparaíso
And my legs in Montreal.

I lost my ears in New York City
And in Trinidad, my hair.
Lost my memory in...
(Now where was it I lost my memory?)
Oh, I can't remember where.

And if that wasn't bad enough
I think I'm losing my voice...

# DAZE OF THE WEEK

On Sunday we saw Paris,
On Monday, Amsterdam.
Tuesday – Barcelona,
Wednesday, Siam.

Thursday was Australia.
Friday we saw Rome.
Saturday was Africa
And then we all came home.

# A ROVING EYE

I have a roving eye.
It swivels round and round.
And when I'm looking at the stars
It's staring at the ground.

I have a roving eye.
No choice in where it goes.
I'll try to look you in the eye
But might look up your nose.

A-roving, a-roving,
I have a roving eye.
It swivels right, it swivels left,
I have a roving eye.

I have a roving eye.
I've no control at all.
It simply won't behave itself.
It drives me up the wall!

## THE SQUIDGEREE

Way down deep
At the bottom of the sea
Lives a marvellous fish
Called the Squidgeree.

It's got no bones
And it's got no skin.
It's got no tail
And it's got no fin.

It's got no mouth
And it's got no eyes.
It tells no secrets,
Tells no lies.

It doesn't eat
And it doesn't swim.
No luminous light,
So it's very dim.

If you approach
With stealth and care,
You'll find the Squidgeree's
Not there.

It's a marvellous fish,
The Squidgeree.
The most marvellous fish
You'll never see.

## LIGHT NIGHTS, NIGHT LIGHTS

I think the sun should be shining at night.
It's *then* that the world and its people need light,
Rather than during the day when we don't.
I'm sure you'll agree, but then maybe you won't.

## TIME WARPED

With the wonders of modern technology
And the latest in warp-factor flight;
If you leave home on Saturday morning
You can get home the previous night.

# ALIENS ON VACATION

They come from planets near and far,
Some big, some small, some quite bizarre.
Twinkle, twinkle, little star –
Aliens on vacation!

They've read the brochures, booked hotels,
Had their shots and said farewells.
Run for cover! Ring them bells!
Aliens on vacation!

Towards the Earth the pilot steers.
They've come to look for souvenirs,
Eat some pizza, drink some beers –
Aliens on vacation!

If you stare, they'll start a fight.
They sing rude songs and dance all night.
They go to bed when it gets light –
Aliens on vacation!

They hog the sunbeds round the pool,
Splash other guests and play the fool.
They write with spray-paint ALIENS RULE!
Aliens on vacation!

They plunder, photograph and scour.
Their spaceship has enormous power.
It takes on board the Eiffel Tower …
Aliens on vacation!

… From Israel, the Wailing Wall!
From London Town, the Albert Hall!
They take Mount Everest from Nepal …
Aliens on vacation!

... Australia, they take Ayers Rock!
From Scotland, they take Lomond Loch!
From England, they take Big Ben's clock ...
Aliens on vacation!

... From New York, the Empire State!
San Francisco, Golden Gate!
Never underestimate –
Aliens on vacation!

With famous landmarks now just blanks,
They check their oil and fill their tanks.
They leave without a word of thanks –
Aliens on vacation!

And as they leave, the aliens cheer
And chuck out empty cans of beer;
"We'll all be back again next year!" –
Aliens on vacation!

There's just one thing they overlook:
That when, next year, they try to book,
The phone just might be off the hook –
To aliens on vacation!

## THAT FUNNY FEELING YOU GET IN RAILWAY TUNNELS

As the train went through the railway tunnel,
the little girl looked up at her mummy and said:
"I've gone all quiet and my voice
has gone funny."
And I knew just what she meant.

## DOWN IN THE DUMPS

I'm down in the dumps
On vacation.
Surrounded by garbage,
That's me.
Some people might say
That it's rubbish.
But it's great
'Cause I'm broke
And it's free!

## PANIC ON TITANIC

I was riding a ship of the desert,
Its name it was Titanic,
I should have been suspicious,
But I'm not a man to panic.

I was riding a ship of the desert,
When I heard a terrible clunk!
I'd run into a sandberg
And my ship of the desert sunk.

# AS I WENT WALKING

As I went walking out one day
I met a man and he did say:
"Fiddle-dee-rollop, fiddle-dee-ree,
Rumpety-ti-doe, rumpety-dee."

As I went walking the following day
I met a fair maid and she did say:
"Whimple, whample, wobble-bum-ho,
Swample, fwample, stickle-back-po."

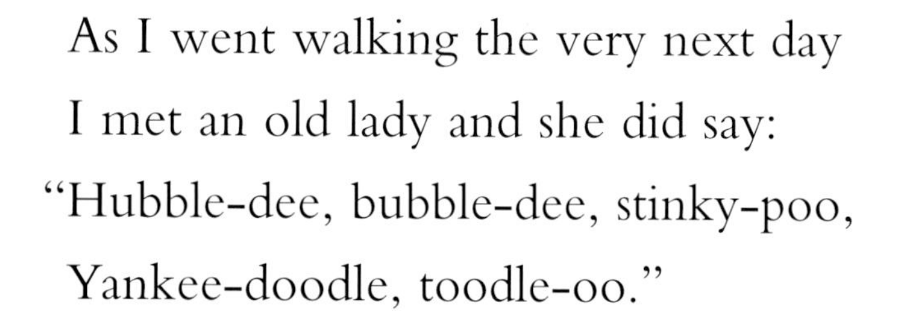

As I went walking the very next day
I met an old lady and she did say:
"Hubble-dee, bubble-dee, stinky-poo,
Yankee-doodle, toodle-oo."

As I went walking on the fourth day
I met a small child and she did say:
"Have you noticed there are some
really weird people around here?"

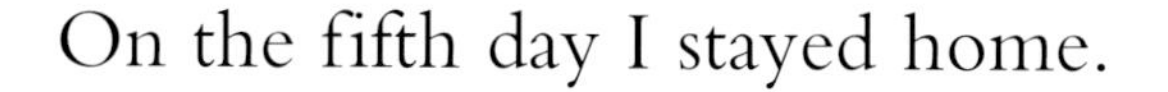

On the fifth day I stayed home.

## A SHORT OLD SAILING POEM

I set off in my sailing boat;
I wore my brand new overcoat.
And had that boat been stronger,
My poem would have been longer.

(And had that coat been lighter,
My future, somewhat brighter.)

## GOING NOWHERE, FAST

I'm going slightly round the twist,
I'm going round the bend.
I'm going round in circles.
I've fallen down. The end.

INDEX

HOTELS
FOOD
BEACHES
WILDLIFE
SEA